Isaiah Baltzell

Carols of praise

A choice collection of new gospel songs, prepared especially for

evangelistic services

Isaiah Baltzell

Carols of praise
*A choice collection of new gospel songs, prepared especially for evangelistic
services*

ISBN/EAN: 9783337266424

Printed in Europe, USA, Canada, Australia, Japan

Cover: Foto ©Thomas Meinert / pixelio.de

More available books at **www.hansebooks.com**

CAROLS OF PRAISE.

—✦—

1.
Salvation is Free.

"And the Spirit and the bride say, Come."—REV. 22: 17.

AMICUS.

I. BALTZELL.

1. O sin-ner, the Saviour is call-ing, He of-fers you par-don now;
2. The world with its pleasures is call-ing, The tempter is seek-ing you;
3. Why lin-ger in paths that are sure-ly Still leading you down to woe?
4. Re-ject the dear Sav-iour no longer, But come and be saved to-day;

Cut loose from the world and its fol-lies, And down at His footstool bow.
O heed not its of-fers of pleasure, But come to the Just and true.
The Saviour is wait-ing to lead you Where rivers of mer-cy flow.
He's a-ble just now to redeem you, And wash all your sins a-way.

CHORUS.

Sal-va-tion is free, Sal-va-tion is free, The
Sal-va-tion is free, Sal-va-tion is free,

Spir-it in-vites you, the Bride says, Come. Sal-va - - - tion is free.
Sal-va-tion, sal-va-tion is free.

2. Whosoever Will.

"Whosoever shall call upon the name of the Lord shall be saved."—ROM. 10: 13.

AMICUS.

I. BALTZELL.

1. Who - so - ev - er will! Shout aloud the sound, Send the gos-pel tidings the
2. Who - so - ev - er comes will a welcome find, For the promise is un - to
3. Who - so - ev - er bows at the Saviour's feet, Shall receive a par-don—a

world around ; Tell the sto-ry sweet, Je-sus is the way; Whoso-ev-er will,
all mankind ; O the blessed news ! hear the Saviour say, Whoso-ev-er will,
rest complete: Sinner, come to Je - sus without de-lay ; Whoso-ev-er will,

CHORUS.

may be saved to-day.   Who - - - so-ev-er, who-so-ev-er will,
may be saved to-day.   Who-so-ev-er will,   who-so-ev-er will,
may be saved to-day.

Who - - - so-ev-er, who-so-ev-er will,   Who - - so-ev-er,
Who-so-ev-er will,   who-so-ev - er will, Who-so-ev-er will,

who-so-ev - er will, Shout the proc-la-ma-tion, who-so-ev - er will!

4

3. The Sanctifying Power.

"The ransomed of the Lord shall return, and come to Zion with songs."—Isa. 35: 10.

R. K. C.   R. Kelso Carter.

1. Oh! glo-ry hal-le-lu-jah, sound the joy-ful strain, Glory to the name of
2. Oh! glo-ry hal-le-lu-jah, let the anthem swell, Glory to the name of
3. Oh! glo-ry hal-le-lu-jah, let His prais-es roll, Glory to the name of
4. Oh! glo-ry hal-le-lu-jah, for the peace within, Glory to the name of

Je - sus, For He par-dons ev-'ry sin and cleanses ev - 'ry stain,
Je - sus, For Christ the Son of God hath conquered death and hell,
Je - sus, For He sends the Ho-ly Ghost and sanc-ti - fies the soul,
Je - sus, For His strength is found in weakness, keeping us from sin,

REFRAIN.

Glo - ry to the name of Je - sus, Glo - ry hal - le - lu - jah!

Glo - ry to His name, There's a sanc-ti - fy - ing pow-er in the

blood of Je - sus Christ, A sanc-ti-fy - ing power, hal - le - lu - jah!

5

4. Believe and Receive.

"The blood of Jesus Christ his Son cleanseth us from all sin."—1 John 1 : 7.

AMICUS.   REV. J. H. VON NEIDA.

1. How sweet are the words of the gos - pel!   O how rich   is the
2. He came   to re—deem all the lost ones   Who were wand'ring in
3. O   why do you tar - ry, dear sin - ner?   Je - sus calls you in
4. There's no oth - er ref - uge, dear sin - ner;   To be saved there is

mes-sage of peace! Proclaiming re-demp-tion in Je - sus, Who hath
darkness be-low;—To give each a home in   His kingdom;—Wea-ry
mer - cy to-day; O think of the love that He gave you. Will you
no oth - er way; Then fly to the ref - uge this mo - ment, He is

died for   the sin-ner's re-lease.
one, to   the dear Sav-iour go.
come, ere He pass-es   a - way?
wait-ing to save you to - day.

CHORUS.

O be-lieve, and re-ceive this sal-

va-tion, That was purchased for you and for me ;   O doubt, then, no more

your re - demp-tion Thro' the blood that was shed   on the tree.

5. **Retreat. L. M.**

Words by H. STOWELL.   Music by T. HASTINGS.

1. From every storm - y wind that blows, From every swell-ing tide of woes,
2. There is a place where Je-sus sheds The oil of glad-ness on our heads—
3. There is a scene where spirits blend, Where friend holds fellowship with friend;
4. There, there on ea - gle wings we soar, And sin and sense molest no more;

There is a calm a sure re-treat, 'Tis found be-neath the mer - cy - seat.
A place of all on earth most sweet, It is the blood-bought mer-cy - seat.
Tho' sundered far, by faith they meet A-round one com-mon mer - cy - seat.
And heav'n comes down our souls to greet, And glory crowns the mer-cy - seat.

6. **Hursley. L. M.**

Words by JOHN KEBLE.   Music by PETER RITTER.

1. Sun of my soul, Thou Sav-iour dear, It is not night if Thou be near;
2. When the soft dews of kind - ly sleep My wearied eye - lids gen - tly steep,
3. A-bide with me from morn till eve, For without Thee I can - not live;
4. Be near to bless me when I wake, Ere thro' the world my way I take;

O may no earth-born cloud a - rise, To hide Thee from Thy servant's eyes.
Be my last thought, how sweet to rest For-ev-er on my Sav-iour's breast.
A-bide with me when night is nigh, For without Thee I dare not die.
A-bide with me till in Thy love, I lose my - self in heav'n a - bove.

7

7. Tenting on the Old Camp Ground.

"How goodly are thy tents, O Jacob, and thy tabernacles, O Israel."—Num. 24: 5.

L. H. P.

L. H. PARTHEMORE.

1. An-oth-er year has passed away; We're tenting on the old camp-ground.
2. Come, brethren, all u-nite and sing, We're tenting on the old camp-ground.
3. The Lord will meet His children here Who're tenting on the old camp-ground.
4. Come, praise the Lord for joy and peace, While tenting on the old camp-ground.

We've met a - gain to sing and pray, While tenting on the old camp-ground.
To Christ your prayers and praises bring, While tenting on the old camp-ground.
He'll fill our hearts with love sincere, While tenting on the old camp-ground.
A few more years, and we shall cease Our tenting on the old camp-ground.

REFRAIN.

We're tenting on the old camp-ground, brother. Tenting on the old camp-ground.

To the Lord we'll raise our songs of praise While tenting on the old camp-ground.

8. Come Back, My Boy.

"And he arose, and came to his father."—LUKE 15: 20.

J. H. W.

REV. J. H. WEBER, by per.

1. Can a boy forget his mother's prayer, When he has wandered, God knows where?
2. Can a boy forget his moth-er's face, Whose heart was kind and filled with grace?
3. Can a boy for - get his mother's door, From which he wandered years before?
4. Can a boy for - get his mother, dead, Tho' many years have quickly fled?

Tho' down the path of death and shame, But mother's prayers are heard the same.
Her lov - ing voice, it echoes sweet; She waits, she longs her boy to meet!
With burning tears she said, "*Good-bye*, Meet me, my boy, be-yond the sky!"
Those tears, that pray'r, that sweet "Good-bye;" She waits to greet that boy on high.

CHORUS.

Come back, my boy, come back to-day, And trav-el in thy mother's way!

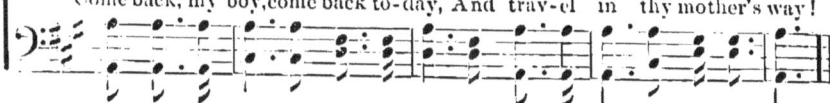

Come back, my boy, come back to-day, And trav-el in thy mother's way!

9. Wholly Thine.

1 I would be, dear Saviour, wholly Thine;
  Teach me how, teach me how;
  I would do Thy will, O Lord! not
  mine;
  Help me, help me now.

REFRAIN.

Wholly Thine, wholly Thine,
  Wholly Thine, this is my vow;
Wholly Thine, wholly Thine,
  Wholly Thine, O Lord! just now.

2 What is worldly pleasure, wealth or
  fame,
  Without Thee, without Thee?
  I will leave them all for Thy dear
  name,
  This my wealth shall be.

3 As I cast earth's transient joys behind,
  Come Thou near, come Thou near;
  In Thy presence all in all I find,
  'Tis my comfort here.

10. He Careth For You.

"Casting all your care upon him; for he careth for you."—1 Pet. 5: 7.

L. H. BAKER.   I. BALTZELL.

1. Child of God, in service faith-ful, Does thy du-ty seem a load?
2. He will com-fort and sustain thee, He will strength and help afford;
3. Cast-ing all your care up-on Him, He will guide you by His word;

Hear the words of love e-ter-nal: "Cast thy bur-den on the Lord."
He will lighten ev-'ry du-ty; "Cast thy bur-den on the Lord."
He will gladden hearts that trust Him; "Cast thy bur-den on the Lord."

CHORUS.

Cast thy burden on the Lord,   Cast thy burden on the Lord,
Cast thy burden on the Lord,   Cast thy burden on the Lord,

Cast thy burden on the Lord,   For He car-eth, He car-eth for you.
Cast thy burden on the Lord,

11. Uxbridge. L. M.

Words by HARRIET AUBER.   Music by LOWELL MASON.

1. Ere mountains reared their forms sublime, Or heaven and earth in order stood ;
2. A thou-sand a-ges in their flight, With Thee are as a fleet-ing day ;
3. But our brief life's a shadowy dream—A passing tho't that soon is o'er—
4. To us, O Lord, the wisdom give Each passing moment so to spend

Be-fore the birth of an-cient time, From ev-er-lasting, Thou art God.
Past, present, future to Thy sight At once their various scenes display.
That fades with morning's earliest beam, And fills the musing mind no more.
That we at length with Thee may live, Where life and bliss shall never end.

12. Ward. L. M.

Words by A. L. HILLHOUSE.   Arr. by LOWELL MASON.

1. Earth has a joy unknown in heav'n—The new-born joy of sins for-giv'n !
2. You saw of old on cha-os rise The beauteous pil-lars of the skies ;
3. Bright heralds of th'E-ter-nal Will Abroad His er-rands you ful-fill ;
4. But I amid your choirs shall shine, And all your knowledge shall be mine ;

Tears of such pure and deep de-light, O an-gels, nev-er dimm'd your sight.
You know where morn exulting springs, And evening folds her drooping wings.
Or, throned in floods of beam-y day, Symphonious in His presence play.
You on your harps must learn to hear A se-cret chord that mine shall bear.

13. Far Away.

"For thou shalt rest, and stand in thy lot."—DAN. 12: 13.

JOHN MCPHERSON.   CHAS. EDW. POLLOCK.

1. Far a - way in the bright land of bliss, Where the spir - its are
2. Far a - way in a sun - ni - er clime, We will bask in the
3. Far a - way, yet how near it may be When we'll sing on that

freed from all care, In a land that is fair - er than this. We a
sun-shine of love, And we'll join in those anthems sub-lime They are
sum - mer-like shore, In a home that is wait-ing for me, Where we'll

CHORUS.

home with the an - gels will share.   Far away,   far a-
sing - ing for - ev - er a - bove.
sor - row and sin nev - er-more.   Far a-way,

way,   Whether far, or near it may be; We shall rest   a-
far away,   We shall rest

mong the blest,   In that land where no sor-row we'll see.
among the blest,

14. Empty Me of Self.

"Lead me in thy truth, and teach me."—Psa. 25: 5.

J. S. N.

Rev. J. S. Norris.

1. Emp-ty me of self, dear Sav - iour, My poor heart re - new;
2. While I cry to Thee, dear Sav - iour, Cleanse me from all sin;
3. Give me Thy own mind, dear Sav - iour, Teach me Thy sweet will;
4. Help me, day by day, dear Sau - iour, Give me strength di - vine;

This great work so wondrous ho - ly, Thou a - lone canst do.
Wash me in the crimson foun-tain, Make me pure with-in.
Fill me with Thy ho - ly Spir - it, Thy blest word ful - fil.
Grant me wis-dom for Thy ser - vice, All Thou hast is mine.

Chorus.

Emp-ty me of self, dear Sav - iour, Help me know Thy love,
loving Saviour,

Bring me when this life is end - ed, To Thy home a-bove,
when this life is end-ed,

Bring me when this life is end - ed, To Thy home a - bove.
when this life is ended,

Used by permission of United Society of Christian Endeavor.

13

15. There's a Shout in the Camp.

"Shout unto God with the voice of triumph."—PSA. 47: 1.

FANNY J. CROSBY.   JNO. B. SWENEY.

1. There's a shout in the camp for the Lord is here, Hal-le-lu-jah! praise His
2. There's a shout in the camp like the shout of old, Hal-le-lu jah! praise His
3. There's a shout in the camp of the King of kings, Hal-le-lu-jah! praise His
4. There's a shout in the camp while our souls re-peat Hal-le-lu-jah! praise His

name;   To the feast of His love we again draw near, Praise, oh,
name;   For the cloud of His glo - ry we now be - hold, Praise, oh,
name;   While we drink at the Rock from the living springs, Praise, oh,
name;   There is room for the world at the Saviour's feet, Praise, oh,

praise His name;

CHORUS.

praise His name. Room for the millions! room for all! Hal-le - lu-jah! praise His

name;   Come to the banquet, great and small, Praise, oh, praise His name.
praise His name;

From "Precious Hymns," by permission of JOHN J. HOOD.

16.

Tell it Again.

"Tell them how great things the Lord hath done."—MARK 5: 19.

Mrs. M. B. C. SLADE.

R. M. McINTOSH.

1. In - to the tent where a gyp - sy boy lay, Dy - ing a - lone at the
2. "Did He so love me,—a poor lit - tle boy? Send un - to me the good
3. Bending we caught the last words of his breath, Just as he en - tered the
4. Smiling, he said, as his last sigh he spent, "I am so glad that for

close of the day, News of sal - va - tion we carried; said he,
tid - ings of joy? Need I not per - ish? my hand will he hold?
val - ley of death; "God sent His Son!"—"who - so - ev - er?" said he;
me He was sent!" Whis - pered, while low sank the sun in the west,

REFRAIN.

"No - bod - y ev - er has told it to me!" Tell it a - gain!
"No - bod - y ev - er the sto - ry has told!"
"Then I am sure that He sent Him to me!"
"Lord, I be - lieve, tell it now to the rest!"

Tell it again? Salvation's sto - ry re - peat o'er and o'er, Till none can

say of the children of men, "No - bod - y ev - er has told me be - fore."

By permission.

15

17. The Cleansing Fountain.

"A fountain opened ... for sin and uncleanness."—ZECH. 13: 1.

WILLIAM COWPER.　　　　　　　　　　　By per. F. A. BLACKMER.

1. There is a fountain fill'd with blood, Drawn from Immanuel's veins,
2. Thou dying Lamb,Thy precious blood, Shall nev-er lose its power,
3. E'er since, by faith,I saw the stream Thy flowing wounds sup-ply,
4. Then in a nobler,sweeter song, I'll sing Thy power to save,

And sinners plung'd beneath that flood Lose all their guilt-y stains.
Till all the ransomed Church of God Are saved,to sin no more.
Re-deem-ing love been my theme, And shall be, till I die.
When this poor,lisping,stammering tongue Lies si-lent in the grave.

CHORUS.

Oh pre-cious foun-tain, cleans-ing stream, Where
Oh pre--cious fountain,cleansing stream,

all may plunge and be made clean; All glo-ry to my Saviour
and be made clean;All glo-ry

be. Who shed His blood to ran-som me.
to my Saviour be, to ransom me.

16

18.   **Evan. C. M.**

Words by J. SWAIN.   Music by H. W. HAVERGAL.

1. How sweet, how heav'nly is the sight When those that love the Lord
2. When each can feel his brother's sigh, And with him bear a part;
3. When free from en - vy, scorn and pride, Our wish - es all a - bove,
4. When love, in the delightful stream, Thro' ev - 'ry bo - som flows;
5. Love is the gold - en chain that binds The hap - py souls a - bove,

In one an - oth - er's peace de - light, And so ful - fill the word.
When sorrow flows from eye to eye, And joy from heart to heart:
Each can his broth - er's fail - ing hide, And show a broth - er's love.
When union sweet, and dear es - teem, In ev - 'ry ac - tion glows.
And he's an heir of heaven, that finds His bo - som glow with love.

19.   **Ortonville. C. M.**

Words by P. DODDRIDGE.   Music by DR. T. HASTINGS.

1. Je - sus! I love Thy charming name, 'Tis music to mine ear ; Fain would I sound it
2. Yes, Thou art precious to my soul, My Transport and my Trust; Jewels to Thee are
3. All that my ardent soul can wish In Thee doth richly meet ; Nor to my eyes is
4. Thy grace shall dwell upon my heart, And shed its fragrance there ;

The noblest balm of

out so loud, That all the earth might hear, That all the earth might hear.
gaud-y toys, And gold is sor - did dust, And gold is sor - did dust.
light so dear, Nor friendship half so sweet, Nor friendship half so sweet.
all its wounds, The cor-dial of its care, The cor-dial of its care.

17

20. Singing Glory to the Lamb!

"Singing with grace in your hearts to the Lord."—Col. 3: 16.

AMICUS.   I. BALTZELL.

1. Let us raise our hearts and voi - ces in a gos - pel song,
2. Gird the gos - pel ar - mor on, and du - ty's call o - bey,
3. On to bat - tle 'neath the ban - ner of the sa - cred cross,
4. We shall sure - ly win the bat - tle by the Ho - ly Word,

Singing glo - ry to the Lamb of God! May the Spir - it of Je -
Singing glo - ry to the Lamb of God! Let us ral - ly to the
Singing glo - ry to the Lamb of God! We will con - quer sin and
Singing glo - ry to the Lamb of God! Let us brave - ly strike for

ho - vah move this mighty throng, Singing glo - ry to the Lamb of God!
conflict—to the field a - way, Singing glo - ry to the Lamb of God!
Sa - tan—counting all but dross, Singing glo - ry to the Lamb of God!
freedom, trusting in the Lord, Singing glo - ry to the Lamb of God!

CHORUS.

O, the chil - dren of the kingdom have a right to shout and sing,

For the way is so de - light - ful, and our souls are on the wing;

We are on our jour-ney homeward to the pal - ace of the King;

Hal - le - lu - jah, hal - le - lu - jah to the Lamb of God!

21. Beautiful Home.

"I go to prepare a place for you."—JOHN 14: 2.

AMICUS.   REV. J. H. VON NEIDA.

1. Beau-ti - ful mansions prepared for me, Prepared for me, prepared for me;
2. Lone-ly and com-fort-less here I roam, Yes, here I roam, yes, here I roam;
3. Light in the dis-tance, by faith I see, By faith I see, by faith I see;
4. Je - sus, I love Thee, I'd love Thee more, I'd love Thee more, I'd love Thee more;
5. Sin-ner, the Sav-iour is call-ing you, Is call-ing you, is call-ing you;

FINE.

Beau-ti - ful cit - y by faith I see:—Sweet home, beau-ti - ful home!
O - ver the riv - er no sorrows come:—Sweet home, beau-ti - ful home!
Sweet is the mu-sic that comes to me:—Sweet home, beau-ti - ful home!
Fol-low Thee on to the golden shore:—Sweet home, beau-ti - ful home!
Will you be lost with this home in view?—Sweet home, beau-ti - ful home!

D.S.—Here in the val - ley my soul can sing, Sweet home, beau-ti - ful home!

CHORUS.   D.S.

Beau-ti - ful home, beau-ti - ful home, Beau-ti - ful, beau-ti - ful home.

beautiful home!

22. He is Just the Same To-day.

"Jesus Christ, the same yesterday, to-day, and forever."—HEB. 13: 8.

Selected.   I. BALTZELL.

1. Have you ev - er heard how Je-sus Walk'd up-on the storm-y sea?
2. Have you ev - er heard the sto - ry Of the Babe of Beth - le - hem?
3. Once while resting on a pil - low, In the ves-sel fast a - sleep,
4. Sure - ly you have heard how Je-sus Prayed in sad Geth-sem - a - ne,—

While the lit - tle ship was toss-ing On the sea of Gal - i - lee;
Who was worshiped by the an-gels And the wise and ho - ly men?
There a - rose a mighty tem-pest, On the wild and an - gry deep;
How he shed his precious life-blood On the Cross of Cal - va - ry—

How he rescued sinking Pe - ter Filled with ter - ror and dis - may;
How he taught the learn-ed doctors In the tem - ple far a - way,
"Peace, be still," the Lord commanded, Ev - 'ry an-gry wave did stay;
How he cried, "Sal-va-tion's finished," As His Spir - it passed a - way;

Wea - ry sin-ner, let me tell you, He is just the same to - day.
Wand'ring sin-ner, let me tell you, He is just the same to - day.
O, I'm glad to tell you, sin-ner, He is just the same to - day.
Come, ye wea-ry, heav - y lad - en, He is just the same to - day.

He is Just the Same To-day.

Concluded.

REFRAIN.

He is just the same to - day, He is just the same to - day,

Oh, sin - ner, let me tell you, He is just the same to - day.

23.   Coronation.   C. M.

Words by E. PERRONET.

Music by O. HOLDEN.

1. All hail the pow'r of Je - sus' name! Let an - gels pros-trate fall:
2. Ye chos-en seed of Is - rael's race—A rem - nant weak and small,—
3. Let ev - 'ry kin-dred, ev - 'ry tribe On this ter - res-trial ball,
4. O that, with yon-der sa - cred throng, We at His feet may fall,

Bring forth the roy - al di - a - dem, And crown Him Lord of all:
Hail Him, who saves you by His grace, And crown Him Lord of all:
To Him all ma - jes - ty ascribe, And crown Him Lord of all:
We'll join the ev - er - last-ing song, And crown Him Lord of all:

Bring forth the roy - al di - a - dem, And crown Him Lord of all.
Hail Him, who saves you by His grace, And crown Him Lord of all.
To Him all ma - jes - ty ascribe, And crown Him Lord of all.
We'll join the ev - er - last-ing song, And crown Him Lord of all.

24. **Jesus Saves Me.**

"He hath put a new song in my mouth, even praises to God."—PSA. 40: 3.

LOUISA M. ROUSE. REV. J. H. VON NEIDA.

1. Precious Sav-iour, Thou hast sav'd me, Thine, and on - ly Thine I am;
2. Long my yearning heart was try - ing To en - joy this per-fect rest;
3. Trusting, trusting ev - 'ry moment; Feel-ing now the blood ap-plied;
4. Con-se - crat - ed to Thy ser-vice, I will live and die to Thee;
5. Glo - ry, glo - ry, Je - sus saves me, Glo - ry, glo - ry to the Lamb!

Oh, the cleansing blood has reach'd me, Glo-ry, glo - ry to the Lamb!
But I gave all try - ing o - ver; Sim-ply trust - ing, I was blest.
Ly - ing at the cleansing fountain; Dwelling at my Saviour's side.
I will wit - ness to Thy glo - ry Of sal - va - tion full and free.
Oh, the cleansing blood has reach'd me, Glo - ry, glo - ry to the Lamb!

CHORUS.

Glo - ry to God! I cannot keep from singing; Glory to God! the gospel bells are

ringing; Sweet the message they are bringing, Je-sus saves me, bless His name!

Copyright, 1891, by I. BALTZELL.

25. Maitland. C. M.

Words by THOMAS SHEPHERD.　　　　　Music by GEO. N. ALLEN.

1. Must Je - sus bear the cross a - lone, And all the world go free?
2. The con - se-cra - ted cross I'll bear, Till death shall set me free;
3. Up - on the crys-tal pavement, down At Je - sus' pierc-ed feet,
4. O pre-cious cross! O glorious crown! O res - ur-rec - tion day!

No, there's a cross for ev - ery one, And there's a cross for me.
And then go home my crown to wear, For there's a crown for me.
With joy I'll cast my gold-en crown, And His dear name re - peat.
Ye an - gels, from the stars come down, And bear my soul a - way.

26. Balerma. C. M.

Words by JOHN NEWTON.　　　　　Music by R. SIMPSON.

1. Ap-proach, my soul, the mer - cy seat, Where Je - sus an-swers prayer;
2. Thy prom-ise is my on - ly plea, With this I ven - ture nigh;
3. Bowed down beneath a load of sin, By Sa - tan sore - ly pressed,
4. Be Thou my shield and hid - ing-place, That, sheltered near Thy side,
5. Oh, wondrous love, to bleed and die, To bear the cross and shame.

There hum-bly fall be-fore His feet, For none can per - ish there.
Thou call - est bur-dened souls to Thee, And such, O Lord, am I.
By war with-out and fear with-in, I come to Thee for rest.
I may my fierce ac - cu - ser face, And tell him "Thou hast died."
That guilt - y sin - ners, such as I, Might plead Thy pre-cious name!

23

27. Will You Come In?

"Him that cometh unto me I will in no wise cast out."—JOHN. 6: 37.

L. A. MORRISON.   J. H. HATHAWAY.

1. The kingdom of heav-en is o - pen to - day; Will you come in?
2. The kingdom of heav-en is waiting to - day; Will you come in?
3. The kingdom of heav-en is pleading to - day; Will you come in?
4. The door of this kingdom will short-ly be closed; Will you come in?

Will you come in? We call from its por - tals, to win you a - way,
Will you come in? We call from its por - tals, why will you de - lay
Will you come in? A - rise, and the voice of en - treat - y o - bey,
Will you come in? Come en - ter in quickly though sin is op-posed,—

Out of the ser-vice of sin, The sunlight and sweetness of
Still in the ser-vice of sin? The Spir-it is call-ing and
Leave the low ser-vice of sin, The mil - i - tant host and the
Break from the ser-vice of sin, The door is still o - pen, no

par - don is here, The love that is per - fect and cast - eth out fear;
so is the Bride, The King has a place for thee close at His side;
ransomed will raise A ju - bi - lant an-them of gladness and praise
lon - ger de - lay, The sum-mer and har-vest are pass-ing a - way;

Will You Come In? Concluded.

$f.$ FINE.

Tho' straight be the gate where its glories appear, There's infinite wideness within.
The gifts of the kingdom Thy coming abide; There's light and rejoicing within.
For one who, repentant, is found in the ways Of Jesus to glo-ry with-in.
O come in the kingdom, dear sinner, to-day, A banquet is waiting within.

D.S.—For Jesus is King, and the kingdom is near; Oh, will you, this moment come in?

CHORUS.   D.S.

Come in! Come in! Will you this mo-ment come in?
Will you come in? Will you come in?

28.   Just as I Am.

CHARLOTTE ELLIOTT.   (Woodworth. L. M.)   WM. B. BRADBURY.

1. Just as I am, with-out one plea, But that Thy blood was shed for me,
2. Just as I am, and waiting not To rid my soul of one dark blot,
3. Just as I am, tho' toss'd a-bout, With many a conflict, many a doubt,
4. Just as I am, poor, wretched, blind, Sight, riches, healing of the mind,
5. Just as I am; Thou wilt receive, Wilt welcome, pardon, cleanse, relieve;

And that Thou bidd'st me come to Thee, O Lamb of God! I come, I come!
To Thee, whose blood can cleanse each spot O Lamb of God! I come, I come!
Fight-ings and fears within, with-out, O Lamb of God! I come, I come!
Yea, all I need in Thee to find, O Lamb of God! I come, I come!
Be - cause Thy prom-ise I be-lieve, O Lamb of God! I come, I come!

2s

29. To Canaan.

"But now they desire a better country, that is an heavenly."—HEB. 11: 16.

MRS. M. B. C. SLADE.   DR. A. BROOKS EVERETT.

SOLO.

1. We are marching to Canaan, thro' the desert vast, And the Lord, with cloud by
2. Tho' we thirst in the des-ert. Thou art ev-er nigh, Giving wa-ters, clear and
3. Green and cool Elim's palm trees, where we peaceful rest, Dewy shelter sweet and
4. When the swelling of Jordan sounds upon the shore, When its parted waves we

day; And the light of His presence, till the night is past, Is shining o'er our way.
sweet;   If we faint on the journey, manna from on high Is falling at our feet.
fair;   There our Shepherd has borne us, on His gentle breast, So loving is His care.
see,   We will sing glad hosannas, joyful passing o'er; We're coming unto Thee.

CHORUS.

To Jor-dan when we come, As we cross the billow's foam, Come Thou

o'er its wave, our Guide to be. We are com-ing, com-ing,

rit.

lead us safe-ly home, Till the shin-ing land we see.

By permission of R. M. McINTOSH.

30. Wand'rer, Come Home.

"Come unto me, all ye that labor and are heavy laden."—Matt. 11: 28.

A. L. BARBAULD.
WM. NICHOL.

1. Come, said Je - sus' sa-cred voice, Come, and make my paths your choice ;
2. Thou who, houseless, sad, for - lorn, Long hast borne the proud world's scorn ;
3. Ye who, tossed on beds of pain, Seek for ease, but seek in vain ;
4. Hith - er come! for here is found Balm that flows for ev - 'ry wound,

I will guide you to your home, Wea-ry wand'rer, hith-er come.
Long hast roam'd the barren waste, Wea-ry wand'rer, hith-er haste.
Ye, by fierc-er an-guish torn, In remorse for guilt who mourn :—
Peace that ev - er shall en - dure, Rest e - ter - nal, sa-cred, sure.

CHORUS.

Weary wand'rer, come just now, He will wash you white as snow !
Weary wand'rer, come just now, He will wash you white as snow ;

At the throne of mercy bow, And the glory of salvation you shall know.
At the throne of mercy bow,

27

31. No Room in Heaven.

"The door was shut."—MATT. 25: 10.

W. O. CUSHING.　　　　　　　　　　　　　　　I. BALTZELL.

1. How sad it would be, if when thou didst call, All hopeless and un - for -
2. How sad it would be, the har - vest all past, The bright summer days all
3. Oh, haste thee, and fly, while mercy is near, Remember the love that he

giv - en, The an - gel that stands at the beau - ti - ful gate, Should
o - ver; To know that the reap - ers had gathered the grain, And
gave you; The love that has sought thee is seek - ing thee still, And

REFRAIN.

answer, No room in heav-en. Sad, sad, sad would it be! No room in
left thee a - lone for-ev - er.
Je - sus now waits to save you.

heav-en for thee! No room, no room, No room in heav-en for

Slow and soft.

thee! No room, no room, No room in heav - en for thee!

Copyright, 1891, by I. BALTZELL.

32.   **Boylston. S. M.**

Words by Benj. Beddome.   Music by Dr. Lowell Mason.

1. Did Christ o'er sin - ners weep, And shall our cheeks be dry! Let
2. The Son of God in tears The wond'ring an - gels see; Be
3. He wept that we might weep—Each sin de - mands a tear; In

tears of pen - i - ten-tial grief Flow forth from ev - 'ry eye.
thou as - ton - ished, O my soul: He shed those tears for thee.
heav'n a - lone no sin is found, And there's no weep - ing there.

33.   **Dennis. S. M.**

Words by John Fawcett.   Music by H. G. Nageli.

1. Blest be the tie that binds Our hearts in Chris-tian love;
2. Be - fore our Fa-ther's throne, We pour our ar - dent pray'rs;
3. We share our mu - tual woes, Our mu - tual bur-dens bear;
4. Tho' oft - en called to part; A - mid these scenes of pain;
5. This glo - rious hope re - vives Our cour - age by the way;

The fel - low-ship of kin - dred minds Is like to that a - bove.
Our fears, our hopes, our aims are one, Our com-forts and our cares.
And oft - en for each oth - er flows The sym - pa - thiz - ing tear.
Yet we shall still be joined in heart, And hope to meet a - gain.
While each in ex - pect - a - tion lives, And longs to see the day.

34.   The Golden Gate.

"Strive to enter in at the strait gate."—LUKE 13: 24.

ANON.   Arranged for this work.

1. There is   a   time we know not when, A point we know not where,
2. Oh! where is that mys-te-rious bourne By which our path is crossed;
3. How far   may we   go on   in   sin? How long will God for-bear?
4. An   an-swer from the skies is   sent: "Ye that from God de-part!

That mark the des-ti-ny of men, To glo-ry or   despair.
Be-yond which, God Him-self hath sworn, That he who goes is lost,
Where does hope end? and where be-gin The con-fines of despair?
While it   is called to-day, re-pent! And hard-en not your heart."

CHORUS.

Then be prepared, Then be prepared To pass thro' the gold-en gate.

He now in-vites, He now in-vites; O come, ere it be too late.

ALTO SOLO.

Is there an-y-one here who is not prepared To en-ter the golden gate?

30

The Golden Gate. Concluded.

How sad it would be to hear Him say, To late to en-ter the gate.

DUET.

Don't let it be said, too late, too late, To en - ter the gold-en gate;

Be read-y, for soon the Lord will close, The beau-ti-ful gold - en gate.

REFRAIN.

The beau-ti-ful gold - en gate, The beau-ti-ful gold - en gate;
The beau-ti-ful, beautiful golden gate, The beau-ti-ful, beautiful golden gate;

Be read-y, for soon the Lord will close The beau-ti-ful golden gate.

31

35. Hallelujah! I Am Saved.

"Thanks be to God, which giveth us the victory."—1 Cor. 15: 57

CLARA TEARE.   I. BALTZELL.

1. All my life - long I have pant - ed For a draught from some cool spring,
2. Feeding on the husks a-round me, Till my strength was al-most gone,
3. Poor I was. and sought for rich - es, Something that would sat-is - fy,
4. Well of wa - ter, ev - er spring-ing. Bread of life, so rich and free,

That I hoped would quench the burning, Of the thirst I felt with - in.
Long'd my soul for something bet - ter, On - ly still to hun-ger on.
But the dust I gath-ered round me, On - ly mock'd my soul's sad cry.
Un-told wealth that nev-er fail - eth, My Re-deem - er is to me.

CHORUS.

Hal - le - lu - jah! I have found Him, Whom my soul so long has craved!

Je - sus sat - is - fies my long-ings ; Thro' His blood I now am saved.

Copyright, 1891, by I. BALTZELL.

36. Would You Know Why I Love Jesus?

1 Would you know why I love Jesus?
  Why He is so dear to me?
  'Tis because my blessed Jesus
  From my sins has ransomed me.

2 Would you know why I love Jesus?
  Why He is so dear to me?
  'Tis because the blood of Jesus
  Fully saves and cleanses me.

3 Would you know why I love Jesus?
  Why He is so near to me?
  'Tis because, amid temptation,
  He supports and strengthens me.

4 Would you know why I love Jesus?
  Why He is so dear to me?
  'Tis because, my Friend and Saviour,
  He will ever, ever be.

32

37. O Grieve Not the Spirit.

AMICUS.

"Grieve not the Holy Spirit of God."—Eph. 4: 30.

I. BALTZELL.

1. The Spir - it is striv - ing, dear sin - ner, to - day, O
2. O wan - der - er, will you from sin - ser - vice cease? The
3. Thy sins which are ma - ny, He'll free - ly for - give, Re -
4. O quench not the Spir - it, the Sav - iour is nigh, To

will you still drive the dear stran-ger a - way? Re-sist not His
Spir - it will fill you with com - fort and peace; From chains that now
pent, guilt-y sin - ner, sal - va - tion re-ceive, For Je - sus is
lift you to man-sions of glo - ry, on high; The Spir - it is

wooings, no lon-ger de - lay; O grieve not the Spir-it of God.
bind you there's certain re - lease; O grieve not the Spir-it of God.
wait-ing thy soul to re - lieve, O grieve not the Spir-it of God.
striving, then why will you die? O grieve not the Spir-it of God.

REFRAIN. Repeat pp.

O grieve not the Spirit, O grieve not the Spirit, O grieve not the Spirit of God.

38. Ho! Every One That Thirsteth.

"I will give unto him that is athirst of the fountain of the water of life freely."—REV. 21: 6.

W. A. OGDEN.   W. A. OGDEN.

1. Ho! ev-ery one that thirst-eth! Come,oh,come ye to the wa-ters,
2. Ho! ev-ery one that thirst-eth! Come,oh,come ye to the wa-ters,
3. Ho! ev-ery one that thirst-eth! Come,oh,come ye to the wa-ters,

FINE. DUET.

Ho! ev-ery one that thirst-eth, Drink and live. Christ hath o-pened
Ho! ev-ery one that thirst-eth, Drink and live. Christ hath of-fered
Ho! ev-ery one that thirst-eth, Drink and live Christ for thee is

CHORUS.   DUET.

up a foun-tain, Drink and live! Yon-der on the sa-cred mountain,
free sal-va-tion, Drink and live! Un-to ev-ery tribe and na-tion,
in-ter-ced-ing, Drink and live! With the Fa-ther He is plead-ing,

CHORUS.   DUET.   CHORUS.

Drink and live! He that hath no mon-ey, Let him come and buy and eat,
Drink and live! He that hath no mon-ey, Let him come and drink and live,
Drink and live! He that hath no mon-ey, Hear the message from the Lord,

34

Ho! Every One That Thirsteth. Concluded.

DUET. *D.C.*

He that hath no mon - ey, Let him take life's wa - ter sweet,
He that hath no mon - ey, Ev - er - last - ing life re - ceive,
He that hath no mon - ey, 'Tis re - cord - ed in His word,

39. Revive Us Again.

"Wilt thou not revive us again."—Psa. 85: 6.

WM. PATON MACKAY. J. J. HUSBAND.

1. We praise Thee, O God! for the Son of Thy love, For Je - sus who
2. We praise Thee, O God! for Thy Spir-it of light, Who has shown us our
3. All glo - ry and praise to the Lamb that was slain, Who has borne all our
4. All glo - ry and praise to the God of all grace, Who has bought us, and
5. Re - vive us a - gain; fill each heart with Thy love; May each soul be re -

REFRAIN.

died, and is now gone a - bove. Hal-le-lu - jah! Thine the glory; Hal-le -
Sav-iour and scattered our night.
sins, and has cleans'd ev'ry stain.
sought us, and guid-ed our ways.
kin-dled with fire from a - bove.

lu - jah! A - men! Hal-le - lu - jah! Thine the glo-ry; re - vive us a - gain.

35

40. Sweet Peace, the Gift of God's Love.

"Peace I leave with you, my peace I give unto you."—JOHN 14 : 27.

P. B.

P. BILHORN. By per.

1. There comes to my heart one sweet strain, A glad and a joy-ous re - frain,
   sweet strain,   re-frain,
2. By Christ on the cross peace was made, My debt by His death was all paid,
   was made,   all paid,
3. When Je - sus as Lord I had crowned, My heart with this peace did abound,
   had crowned,   abound,
4. In Je - sus for peace I a-bide, abide, And as I keep close to His side, His side,

I sing it a - gain and a - gain, Sweet peace, the gift of God's love.
No oth - er foun-da-tion is laid For peace, the gift of God's love.
In Him the rich blessings I found, Sweet peace, the gift of God's love.
There's nothing but peace doth betide, Sweet peace, the gift of God's love.

CHORUS.

Peace, peace, sweet peace! Won - der - ful gift from a - bove! above! Oh,

rit.

won-der-ful, won-der-ful peace! Sweet peace, the gift of God's love!

41. **Laban. S. M.**

Music by L. MASON.

1. My soul, be on thy guard, Ten thou-sand foes a - rise;
2. Oh, watch, and fight, and pray, The bat - tle ne'er give o'er;
3. Ne'er think the vic - t'ry won, Nor lay thine arm - or down;
4. Fight on, my soul, till death Shall bring thee to thy God;

The hosts of sin are press-ing hard To draw thee from the skies.
Re - new it bold-ly ev - 'ry day, And help di - vine im-plore.
Thy arduous work will not be done Till thou ob - tain the crown.
He'll take thee, at thy part-ing breath Up to His blest a - bode.

42. **St. Thomas. S. M.**

Words by WM. HAMMOND.

Music by A. WILLIAMS.

1. A-wake, and sing the song Of Mo - ses and the Lamb;
2. Sing of His dy - ing love; Sing of His ris - ing power;
3. Sing on your heaven-ly way, You ran - somed sin - ners, come;
4. Soon shall you hear Him say, "You bless - ed chil-dren, come!"

Wake, ev - 'ry heart and ev - 'ry tongue, To praise the Sav-iour's name.
Sing how He in - ter-cedes a - bove, For those whose sins He bore.
Sing on, re - joic-ing ev - 'ry day, In Christ, the glo - rious King.
Soon will He call you hence a - way, And take His pil-grims home.

43. Tell the News.

"Go ye into all the world, and preach the gospel to every creature."—MARK 16: 15.

ANON.   I. BALTZELL.

1. Tell the news of Jesus' love, Tell the news, (tell the news,) How He
2. Lost in sin were all mankind—Tell the news, (tell the news,) Naked,
3. Came to free us from all guilt—Tell the news, (tell the news,) On the
4. Glo-ry to Immanuel's name! Tell the news, (tell the news,) Precious

left His home above—Tell the news, (tell the news,) How He left His Father's throne,
poor, and sick, and blind—Tell the news, (tell the news,) But the great Physician came,
cross His blood was spilt—Tell the news, (tell the news,) Came to heal the wounds of sin,
truth—the Saviour came. Tell the news, (tell the news,) Shout aloud, Salvation's free!

That He might for sin atone, Suffered on the cross a-lone—Tell the news!
Came to heal the sick and lame; "Jesus," "Saviour," is His name—Tell the news!
Came to make us pure within; Came to wash, and make us clean—Tell the news!
Sin-ner, yes, for you, for me! Now, and to e-ter-ni-ty —Tell the news!

CHORUS.

Tell the news,   Tell the news,   O, ye
   The bless-ed news,   The bless-ed news,

38

Tell the News. Concluded.

ransomed of the Lord, Tell the news, (tell the news,) Jesus died on Cal-va-ry,

To a-tone for you and me; Tell the news, (tell the news,) Tell the news!

44. Jesus Saves Me All The Time.

"But Christ is all and in all."—Col. 3: 11.

JAS. NICHOLSON.   J. A. DUNCAN.

1. Je - sus saves me ev - 'ry day, Je - sus saves me ev - 'ry night;
2. Je - sus saves when I re - pine, Je - sus saves when I re - joice;
3. Je - sus saves me, He is mine; Je - sus saves me, I am His;
4. Je - sus saves, He saves from sin, Je - sus saves, I feel Him nigh;

Je - sus saves me all the way— Thro' the dark - ness, thro' the night.
Je - sus saves when hopes de - cline— Faith can al - ways hear His voice.
Je - sus saves while I re - cline— On His pre - cious prom - i - ses.
Je - sus saves, He dwells with - in, Glad - ly do I tes - ti - fy.

CHORUS.

Je - sus saves, O bliss sub - lime— Je - sus saves me all the time.

45. Are You Ready for His Coming?

"At midnight there was a cry made, Behold, the bridegroom cometh."—MATT. 25: 6.

L. J. B.   I. BALTZELL.

1. Are you read-y, friend, to meet Him Who has done so much for you?
2. Are you read-y, friend, to meet Him? Are your treas-ures all a-bove?
3. Are you read-y, friend, to meet Him Should He call for you to-night?

Are you read-y, friend, to greet Him When He comes and calls for you?
Are you read-y, friend, to greet Him Who is Truth, and Life, and Love?
Are you read-y, friend, to greet Him Should He come in morn-ing light?

Life is short and time is pass-ing, Nev-er to re-turn a-gain;
Is your lamp all trimm'd and burning With a clear and cer-tain glow?
Have you lived for Christ, the Saviour—Lived an earnest life and true?

All a-round us they are go-ing From a-mong the sons of men.
All a-round us they are go-ing; Are you read-y, friend, to go?
All a-round us they are go-ing; Soon He'll come and call for you.

CHORUS.

Are you ready, for the Bridegroom, Are you ready, for the Bridegroom, When He comes to gather

40

Are You Ready for His Coming? Concluded.

all His children home, Are your lamps all trimmed and burning, Do you
children home,

wait your Lord's returning; Are you ready for the Bridegroom when He comes?
when He comes?

46. Jesus Saves.

"He shall save his people from their sins."—MATT. 1 : 21.

REV. ALFRED J. HOUGH. CHAS. EDW. POLLOCK.

1. Ma - ny at the cross are kneel-ing, Je - sus, Je - sus saves;
2. Hearts are at this mo - ment pray-ing, Je - sus, Je - sus saves;
3. Hal - le - lu - jah, saints are sing-ing, Je - sus, Je - sus saves;

FINE.

By His boundless love re - veal-ing, Je - sus, Je - sus saves.
Ev - 'ry sin - ful stain re - mov-ing, Je - sus, Je - sus saves.
Heav'n with joy-ous song is ring-ing, Je - sus, Je - sus saves.

D.S.—Hal-le - lu - jah, shout ho - san - na, Je - sus, Je - sus saves.

CHORUS. D.S.

Hal - le - lu - jah, love is beaming, Hal-le - lu - jah, light is streaming,

47. O the Saving Power of Jesus.

"It is the power of God unto salvation to every one that believeth."—ROM. 1: 16.

AMICUS.   I. BALTZELL.

1. Hal - le - lu - jah! Je - sus saves me! I am wash'ed in blood di - vine,
2. Hal - le - lu - jah! Je - sus saves me! I am His, and He is mine;
3. Hal - le - lu - jah! Je - sus saves me! O the won-ders of His grace!
4. Hal - le - lu - jah! Je - sus saves me! I was lost, but now I'm found;

I have found a full sal - va-tion; Now I feel that Christ is mine.
O the bless-ed love that fills me! I shall nev - er-more re - pine.
Free sal-va-tion! flow-ing fountain! For the lost of Adam's race.
I was blind, but now I'm see-ing! Glo-ry! glo-ry! all a-round.

CHORUS.

O the sav-ing power of Je - sus! Now I feel the blood ap-plied;

I have found a full sal - va-tion! And my soul is sat - is - fied.

48. All to Thee, O Blessed Saviour.

1 All to Thee, O blessed Saviour,
From this moment I resign;
All with cheerful heart I give Thee
Let me now be wholly Thine,
All to Thee, all to Thee,
Lord, I give my all to Thee.

2 All to Thee, O blessed Saviour,
I would yield to Thy control;
All to Thee, yes, soul and body,
Now, just now, possess me whole,
All to Thee, all to Thee,
Lord, I give my all to Thee.

49. Rock of Ages. 7s.

Words by A. M. TOPLADY.

Music by THOS. HASTINGS.

FINE.

1. Rock of A - ges, cleft for me, Let me hide my-self in Thee;
D. C.—Be of sin the double cure—Cleanse me from its guilt and power.

Let the wa - ter and the blood, From Thy riv - en side which flowed,

D.C.

2 Not the labor of my hands
Can fulfill the law's demands;
Could my zeal no respite know,
Could my tears forever flow,
All for sin could not atone—
Thou must save and Thou alone.

3 Nothing in my hand I bring;
Simply to Thy cross I cling;
Naked, come to Thee for dress;

Helpless, look to Thee for grace;
Foul, I to the fountain fly;
Wash me, Saviour, or I die.

4 While I draw this fleeting breath,
When my heart strings break in death,
When I soar to worlds unknown,
See Thee on Thy judgment throne,
Rock of Ages cleft for me,
Let me hide myself in Thee.

50. Guide. 7s.

Words by M. M. WELLS. Alt.

Music by M. M. WELLS.

FINE.

1. { Bless - ed Je - sus, faithful Guide, Ev - er near the Christian's side, }
   { Gent - ly lead us by the hand, Pil - grims in a des - ert land, }
D.C.—Whisper soft - ly, Wanderer, come; Fol - low me: I'll guide thee home.

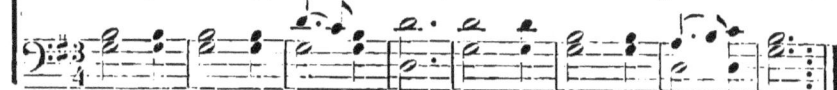

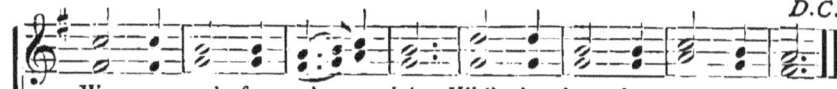

Wea - ry souls for - e'er re - joice, While they hear that sweet - est voice,

D.C.

2 Ever present, truest Friend,
Ever near, Thine aid to lend,
Leave us not to doubt and fear,
Grooping on in darkness drear;
When the storms are raging sore,
Hearts grow faint and hopes give o'er,
Whisper softly, Wanderer, come;
Follow me, I'll guide thee home.

3 When our days of toil shall cease,
Waiting still for sweet release,
Nothing left but heaven and prayer,
Wondering if our names are there;
Wading deep the dismal flood,
Pleading naught but Jesus' blood,
Whisper softly, Wanderer come;
Follow me: I'll guide thee home.

43

51. Christ is Waiting to Save.

"Come, for all things are now ready."—LUKE 14: 17.

Adapted.   I. BALTZELL.

1. Sin-ner, why do you lin-ger in dark-ness so long? Christ is
2. Leave the broad road of sin, and the nar-row way choose, Christ is
3. Time will sure-ly not lin-ger! how soon you must go, Christ is
4. Hear Him call-ing, dear sin-ner, "O, come un-to me, I am
5. While His children are pray-ing, O, stay not a-way, Christ is

wait-ing to save you to-day! Won't you come in this mo-ment and
wait-ing to save you to-day! Ho-ly an-gels are wait-ing to
wait-ing to save you to-day! Sin-ner, why do you halt, and to
wait-ing to save you to-day! I have purchased your par-don, sal-
wait-ing to save you to-day! Will you come in this mo-ment, no

join in the song? Christ is wait-ing to save you to-day!
tell the glad news, Christ is wait-ing to save you to-day!
Je-sus say, "No?" He is wait-ing to save you to-day!
va-tion is free; I am wait-ing to save you to-day!"
lon-ger de-lay; Christ is wait-ing to save you to-day!

CHORUS.

Come, poor sinner, come, come a-way; Come, poor sinner,
Come, come away,   Come, come away.

Christt is Waiting to Save. Concluded.

Come, come to - day, Je - sus is call - ing you, oh,

why do you wait? Re - mem-ber, to - mor-row, it may be too late.

52. Saved by Grace.

"By grace we are saved."—EPH. 2: 8.

W. A. OGDEN.   W. A. OGDEN. By per.

Andante.

1. Saved by grace, oh, bless-ed tid-ings, Won-der-ful His love to show,
2. Saved by grace, oh, bless-ed tid-ings, Je - sus drank the cup for me,
3. Saved by grace, oh, bless-ed tid-ings, Hap-py he who can re-peat,
4. Saved by grace, I'll sing for - ev - er, Tell the wond'rous news a-broad,

Je - sus died to bring sal - va - tion To the per - ish-ing be - low.
Bow'd His head and cried, "'Tis finished," Now my soul is count-ed free.
Who can sing re-demp-tion's sto - ry, Sit-ting at the Saviour's feet.
Spread the gos-pel tid-ings ev - er, Worthy is the Lamb of God.

REFRAIN.

Saved by grace, thro' Je - sus' blood, Made an heir and child of God.

45

53. **Gospel Invitation.**

"Come unto me, all ye that labor and are heavy laden, and I will give you rest."—MATT. 11 : 28.

C. ELLIOTT.   Arranged.

1. With tearful eyes I look around; Life seems a dark and stormy sea,
2. It tells me of a place of rest; It tells me where my soul may flee;
3. "Come," for all else must fail and die! Earth is no rest-ing-place for thee;
4. O voice of mer-cy! voice of love! In con-flict, grief, and ag-o-ny;

Yet, 'mid the gloom, I hear a sound. A heav'nly whisper, "Come to me."
O, to the weary, faint, opprest, How sweet the bidding, "Come to me."
To heav'n di-rect thy weeping eye, I am thy portion, "Come to me."
Support me, cheer me from a-bove, And gently whis-per. "Come to me."

CHORUS.

"Come to me, come to me;" Hear the sweet voice of the Mas-ter saying,

"Come to me, come to me," Wea-ry wand'rer, "Come to me."

54. **Return, and Come to God.**

1 Return, and come to God,
    Cast all your sins away;
Seek ye the Saviour's cleansing blood;
    Repent, believe, obey!

2 Say not ye cannot come,
    For Jesus bled and died,
That none who ask in humble faith
    Should ever be denied.

3 Say not ye will not come;
    'Tis God vouchsafes to call;
And fearful will their end be found,
    On whom His wrath shall fall.

4 Come, then, whoever will;
    Come, while 'tis called to-day;
Seek ye the Saviour's cleansing blood;
    Repent, believe, obey.

55. He Ransomed Me.

STEELE.

"Who gave himself a ransom for all."—1 Tim. 2:6.

I. BALTZELL.

1. And did the Ho-ly and the Just,—The Sov'reign of the skies,—
2. Yes, the Re-deem-er left His throne, His ra-diant throne on high—
3. He took the dy-ing traitor's place, And suffered in his stead;
4. O Lord, what heavenly won-ders dwell In Thine a-ton-ing blood!

Stoop down to wretchedness and dust, That guilt-y man might rise?
Sur-pris-ing mer-cy! love unknown!—To suf-fer, bleed and die.
For sin-ful man—O wondrous grace!—For sin-ful man He bled.
By this are sin-ners saved from hell, And reb-els brought to God.

CHORUS.

He ransomed me, He ransomed me, My Saviour
He ransomed me, He ransomed me,

died to ransom me; He ransomed me, He ransomed
My Saviour died to ransom me; He ransomed me,

me, By His own blood He ransomed me.
He ransomed me, By His own blood He ransomed me.

47

56. # Christ is All.

"Unto you therefore which believe he is precious."—1 Pet. 2: 7.

W. A. Williams.

Effective as a Solo. Ad lib.

1. I entered once a home of care, For age and pen-u-ry were there,
2. I stood beside a dy-ing bed, Where lay a child with ach-ing head,
3. I saw the mar-tyr at the stake, The flames could not his courage shake,
4. I saw the gos-pel her-ald go,—To Afric's sand and Greenland's snow,

Yet peace and joy with-al; I asked the lone-ly moth-er whence
Waiting for Je-sus' call; I marked his smile, 'twas sweet as May,
Nor death his soul ap-pall, I asked him whence his strength was given,
To save from Sa-tan's thrall, Nor home nor life he count-ed dear,

Her helpless wid-ow-hood's de-fense, She told me, "Christ was all."
And as his spir-it passed a-way, He whispered, "Christ is all."
He looked tri-umph-ant-ly to heaven, And answered, "Christ is all."
'Midst wants and perils owned no fear, He felt that "Christ is all."

CHORUS.

Christ is all, all in all, Yes, Christ is all in all: Yes, Christ is all in all.

5 I dreamed that hoary time had fled,
  And earth and sea gave up their dead,
    A fire dissolved this ball,
  I saw the church's ransomed throng,
  I heard the burden of their song,
    'Twas "Christ is all in all."

6 Then come to Christ, oh, come to-day,
  The Father, Son, and Spirit say ;
    The Bride repeats the call,
  For He will cleanse your guilty stains,
  His love will soothe your weary pains,
    For "Christ is all in all."

By permission.

57. Hendon. 7s.

Words by J. MONTGOMERY.

Music by MALAN.

1. Songs of praise awoke the morn
When the Prince of Peace was born ;
Songs of praise a -

rose when he Captive led cap-tiv - i - ty, Captive led cap - tiv - i - ty.

2 Heav'n and earth must pass away—
Songs of praise shall crown the day ;
God will make new heav'ns and earth—
Songs of praise shall hail their birth.

3 Saints below. with heart and voice,
Still in songs of praise rejoice,

Learning here by faith and love,
Songs of praise to sing above.

4 Borne upon the latest breath,
Songs of praise shall conquer death,
Then, amidst eternal joy,
Songs of praise their pow'rs employ.

58. Horton. 7s.

Words by S. LONGFELLOW.

Music by WARTENSEE.

1. Love for all! and can it be?   Can I hope it is   for me—
2. I,   the dis - o - be-dient child,   Wayward, pas - sion-ate   and wild ;
3. I,   who spurn'd His lov-ing hold ;   I, who would not be   controlled ;
4. To   my Fa - ther can I go?   At His feet my-self   I'll throw ;
5. See ! my Fa - ther waiting stands ;   See ! He reach-es   out   His hands :

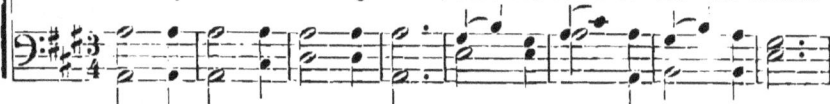

I, who stray'd so   long   a - go,   Stray'd so far, and fell   so low?
I, who left   my   Fa - ther's home,   In   for-bid - den ways to roam ;
I, who would not   hear His call ;   I,   the will - ful prod - i - gal—
In His house there yet   may be   Place—a servant's place—for me.
God is love ; I   know, I   see,   Love for me—yes, e - ven me.

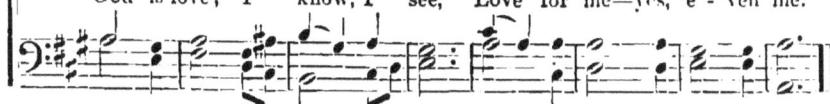

59. Him That Cometh.

"Him that cometh to me I will in no wise cast out."—JOHN 6: 37.

AMICUS.

I. BALTZELL.

1. O sin - ner, the Sav - iour is call - ing, In ac - cents of
2. O wea - ry one, come un - to Je - sus, And seek your sal -
3. Ye thirst - y ones, come to the foun - tain, Still flow - ing so
4. Then hear ye the words of the Sav - iour, And bear - ing O,

mer - cy and love; He's wait - ing this mo - ment to save you—To
va - tion to - day; The gate to the foun - tain is o - pen; No
full and so free; Ye hun - gry, come feed on His boun - ty, There's
nev - er - more doubt, "To him who in pen - i - tence com - eth, I'll

fit you for mansions a - bove.
lon - ger your com - ing de - lay.
plenty for you and for me.
nev - er, no, nev - er cast out."

CHORUS.

Him that cometh to me,

Him that cometh to me,

Him that com - eth to me   I will in no - wise,

Him that com - eth to me,

I will in no - wise, I will in no - wise cast out.

50

60. The Volunteer's Song.

"He wandereth abroad for bread, saying, Where is it?"—Job 15: 23.

R. K. C.

R. KELSO CARTER.

1. A cry comes up from the dark-ness, A wail of ag - o - ny rolls
2. Oh, who can tell this sal - va - tion? The judgment thun - der rolls;
3. Oh, who will go to the res - cue? The world mere pit-tan-ces doles;
4. From east to west we will tell it, To all men between the poles;

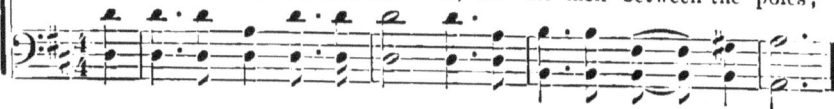

Thro' the night of sin, in this world of ours, 'Tis the cry of per-ish-ing souls.
Who will bear the news of redemption down To the helpless per-ish-ing souls.
'Tis the Christian saved by redeeming love Who must help the per-ish-ing souls.
We can tell it best, we who feel it most, For we once were per-ish-ing souls.

Chorus.

Are you saved? ful-ly saved? Has Jesus wash'd your sins away, away?
Are you saved? ful-ly saved?

Then work, brother, work; the night is coming on; Oh, work, work for souls to-day.

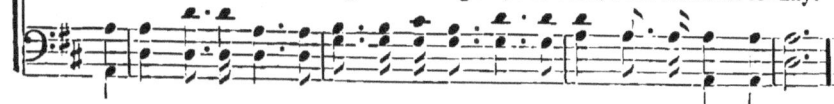

61. What Shall Our Record Be?

"And the books were opened."—Rev. 20; 12.

F. M. D.

Frank M. Davis.

Solo and Chorus.

1. There's a hand that's writ-ing now   In the book of life, they say;
2. Still that hand goes writ-ing on,   Mak-ing pa - ges dark or fair;
3. Time is ebb - ing fast a - way,   Life for us will soon be done;

Ev - 'ry ac - tion, word or deed   Is re - cord - ed there each day.
Let us pon - der well, dear friend,   What for us is writ - ten there.
Can we trust - ing-ly go hence,   That a crown of life is won?

What shall then our rec - ord be?   Let us stop and think I pray!

What shall then our rec - ord be   In the coming judgment day?

Chorus.

In the com-ing judgment day, in the com-ing judg-ment day,

What Shall Our Record Be? Concluded.

What shall then our rec - ord be, In the com-ing judgment day.

62.   I Gave My Life For Thee.

"So Christ was once offered to bear the sins of many."—HEB. 9: 28.

FRANCIS R. HAVERGAL.   Arranged for this work.

1. I gave my life for thee, My precious blood I shed, That thou might'st ransom'd
2. My Father's house of light, My glo-ry circled throne, I left for earthly
3. I suffered much for thee, More than thy tongue can tell, Of bit-ter-est ago -
4. And I have brought to thee, Down from my home above, Sal - va-tion full and

be, And quickened from the dead ; I gave my life for thee,   What
night, For wand'rings sad and lone, I left it all for thee,   Hast
ny, To res - cue thee from hell ; I've borne it all for thee,   What
free, My par-don and my love ; I bring rich gifts to thee, What hast thou

hast thou given for me? I gave my life for thee,   What hast thou given for me?
thou left aught for me? I left it all for thee,   Hast thou left aught for me?
hast thou borne for me? I've borne it all for thee,   What hast thou borne for me?
brought   to   me? I bring rich gifts to thee, What hast thou brought to me?

53

63. I Am Satisfied With Jesus.

"The Lord is my defense, and my God is the Rock of my refuge."—Psa 91: 22.

ANNA CHICHESTER.   JOHN TIBBALLS.

1. I am walking with the Saviour in the bless-ed nar-row way, I am
2. In my griefs He's con-so-la-tion, and in tri - al He's my stay, I am
3. Oh, the words of love and comfort! Oh, the ten-der, lov-ing hand! I am

f.

sat - is-fied with Christ my Lord; Once my soul was in the darkness, Now has
sat - is-fied with Christ my Lord; With His ten-der arms around me I can
sat - is-fied with Christ my Lord; Thro' the wa-ters it will lead me to the

D.S.—nev-er will forsake me, but will
FINE.

dawn'd life's golden day, I am sat - is - fied with Christ my Lord.
nev - er know dis-may, I am sat - is - fied with Christ my Lord.
fair Lamb-lighted land, I am sat - is - fied with Christ my Lord.

ev - er be my Guide, I am sat - is - fied with Christ my Lord.

CHORUS.

I am sat - is-fied, (with Jesus,) Yes, I am sat - is - fied, (with Jesus,)

D.S.

I am sat - is-fied to walk with Him the long, long way; For He

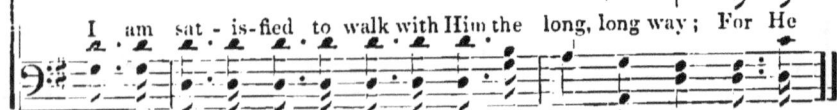

64. **Nettleton.** **8s & 7s.**

REV. R. ROBINSON, 1758.

Old Melody, 1812.

FINE.

1. { Come, Thou Fount of ev-ery bless-ing, Tune my heart to sing Thy grace; }
{ Streams of mer-cy nev-er ceas-ing, Call for songs of loud-est praise; }
D.C.—Praise the mount—I'm fixed upon it! Mount of Thy re-deem-ing love.

D.C.

Teach me some mel-o-dious sonnet, Sung by flaming tongues above;

2 Here I'll raise my Ebenezer,
Hither by Thy help I'm come;
And I hope by Thy good pleasure,
Safely to arrive at home.
Jesus sought me when a stranger,
Wandering from the fold of God;
He to rescue me from danger,
Interposed His precious blood.

3 Oh, to grace how great a debtor,
Daily I'm constrained to be!
Let Thy goodness as a fetter,
Bind my wandering heart to Thee;
Prone to wander, Lord, I feel it—
Prone to leave the God I love—
Here's my heart, oh, take and seal it,
Seal it for Thy courts above.

65. **New Haven.** **6s & 4s.**

REV. RAY PALMER, D. D., 1830.

DR. THOS. HASTINGS, 1833.

1. My faith looks up to Thee, Thou Lamb of Cal-va-ry;
2. May Thy rich grace im-part Strength to my faint-ing heart;

Sav-iour, di-vine; Now hear me while I pray; Take all my
My zeal in-spire; As Thou hast died for me. O may my

guilt a-way; O let me, from this day, Be whol-ly Thine.
love to Thee Pure, warm, and changeless be— A liv-ing fire.

3 While life's dark maze I tread,
And griefs around me spread,
Be Thou my guide;
Bid darkness turn to day;
Wipe sorrow's tears away,
Nor let me ever stray
From Thee aside.

4 When ends life's transient dream;
When death's cold sullen stream
Shall o'er me roll;
Blest Saviour, then in love,
Fear and distress remove;
O bear me safe above,—
A ransom'd soul.

66. Redeemed! Redeemed!

"And hast redeemed us to God by thy blood."—Rev. 5: 9

AMICUS.

I. BALTZELL.

1. I've long been a sin - ner, but now I can sing,
2. I'm go - ing to glo - ry, to join the glad band,
3. A crown of bright glo - ry is wait - ing for me,
4. Ye chil - dren of Je - sus now raise the sweet song,

Redeemed by the blood of the Lamb! All glo - ry to God! I'm a
Redeemed by the blood of the Lamb! For millions have gathered in
Redeemed by the blood of the Lamb! And not for me on - ly, but
Redeemed by the blood of the Lamb! And sing hal - le - lu - jah with

child of the King. Redeemed by the blood of the Lamb!
yon - der bright land, Redeemed by the blood of the Lamb!
all who are free. Redeemed by the blood of the Lamb!
ju - bi - lant tongue, Redeemed by the blood of the Lamb!

D. S.—deemed by the blood of the Lamb!

REFRAIN.

Redeemed! Redeemed! Redeemed by the blood of the
by the blood, by the blood, by the blood,

Lamb! D.S.

blood of the Lamb! Now all the day long I can sing the glad song. Re-

67. Come Home, Poor Sinner.

"So Christ was once offered to bear the sins of many."—HEB. 9: 28.

ANON.

I. BALTZELL.

1. Thy sins I bore on Calvary's tree ;The stripes thy due were laid on me,
2. Burden'd with guilt,would'st thou be blest?Trust not the world;it gives no rest;
3. Come, leave thy burden at the cross;Count all thy gains but empty dross,
4. Come, hith - er bring thy boding fears, Thy aching heart,thy bursting tears,

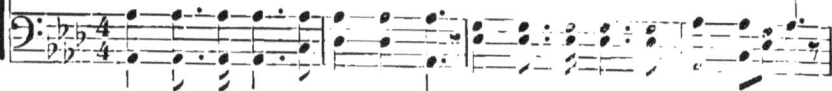

That peace and pardon might be free—O poor,wretched sinner,come home.
I bring re-lief to hearts opprest—O poor, wea-ry sinner,come home.
My grace repays all earth-ly loss—O poor, need-y sinner,come home.
'Tis mercy's voice sa-lutes thine ears ;O poor,trembling sinner,come home.

CHORUS.

Come home, come home, A happy welcome waits you in your
Come home,come home,come home,come home,

Father's house,Come home,come home,O poor,weary sinner,come home.
Come home,come home,come home,come home.

68. He Saved a Sinner Like Me.

"Wherefore he is able to save to the uttermost."—HEB. 7: 25.

AMICUS.

I. BALTZELL.

1. I will sing of the mer-cy of God— Of His won-der-ful
2. Long I wandered in darkness a-lone, Not a ray of
3. Now I walk in the light of His love, For the light is now
4. Soon the jour-ney of life will be o'er, And the dear bless-ed

death on the tree; How He suf-fered and bled, and the
light could I see; O the an-guish and pain, as I
shin-ing on me; And to oth-ers I tell, how He
Je-sus I'll see! On the ev-er-green shore I will

thorns crown'd His head To save a poor sin-ner like me.
strug-gled in vain To find hope for a sin-ner like me.
saved me from hell. And can save oth-er sin-ners like me.
sing ev-er-more, Je-sus saved a poor sin-ner like me.

CHORUS.

He saved a poor sinner like me. He saved a poor sinner like me,
He saved a poor sinner like me,   He saved a poor sinner like me,

All glory and praise to the Ancient of Days! He saved a poor sinner like me.

58

69. The Roll Call.

Words Arranged.

A. T. GORHAM.

A dying soldier suddenly roused up and exclaimed, "Here!" "What do you wish?" asked the surgeon "Nothing," was the reply, "only it was the roll call in glory, and I was answering to my name."

1. When the roll is called in glo-ry, And earth's hosts shall muster there,
2. Tho' my dust lie in the val-ley, Or be-neath the o-cean deep,
3. He who keeps the keys of ha-des Speaks, and lo! the vaulted door
4. Born to life of endless beauty, Sat-is-fied my weary soul,

I will take my place among them, And their joys and triumphs share.
Call the roll and I will wak-en From my dark and dreamless sleep.
Swings ajar— the chains are riven, And His ransomed die no more.
I shall join the glad ho-san-nas When the an-gels call the roll.

Chorus.

Angels call the roll in glo-ry, Muster day for saints proclaim:

Call the roll and at the summons I will an-swer to my name.

70. Whiter Than the Snow.

"Though your sins be as scarlet, they shall be white as snow."—ISA. 1: 18.

ANON.

I. B.

1. From Zi-on's sa - cred mountain see The liv-ing wa - ters glide;
2. That sa - cred fountain filled with blood, Lies o - pen night and day;
3. This fountain cleanses from all sin, And pu - ri - fies the soul;
4. "Ho! ev - 'ry one," the proph-et cries, For ev - 'ry one there's room;

Fly to that foun-tain, fly with me, And plunge beneath the tide.
All who will plunge be-neath the flood Wash all their sins a - way.
Yes, Je - sus' blood will keep us clean, And sanc-ti - fy the whole.
"Ho! ev-'ry one," my soul re-plies, "Now to the fountain come."

CHORUS.

O the blood, that flow'd from Jesus' side! 'Tis an ev - - er flowing
O the blood, 'Tis an ev-er

crim-son tide! Plunge in to-day, and you shall know, It can wash you

whiter than the snow, Whiter than the snow, (yes) whiter than the snow, (yes)

Copyright, 1891, by I. BALTZELL.

Whiter Than the Snow. Concluded.

Whiter than the snow, (yes) whiter than the snow; Plunge in to-
day, and you shall know, It can wash you whiter than the snow.

71. Shall We Pray For You?

E. E. HEWITT.   JNO. R. SWENEY.

1. { When we come with burdened souls And be-fore our Fa-ther bow,
   { Shall we pray for you, dear friend? Shall we plead for you just now? }
2. { Shall we ask a liv-ing faith, And a new and bet-ter heart?
   { That the Ho-ly Spir-it now May re-new-ing grace im-part? }

CHORUS.

Shall we pray for you? While our heart pe-ti-tions blend,
for you?
Com-ing in the Saviour's name, Shall we pray for you, dear friend?

3 Are you willing we should know   4 Come and join us in our prayer;
   That you long for peace within?   Low before the Saviour bow;
Do you seek the Lord indeed,   While He waits to hear your voice,
   And the power that saves from sin?   Give yourself to Jesus now.

72.

1 I love to tell the story
Of unseen things above,
Of Jesus and His glory,
Of Jesus and His love,
I love to tell the story,
Because I know 'tis true;
It satisfies my longings
As nothing else can do.

CHO.—I love to tell the story—
'Twill be my theme in glory,
To tell the old, old story
Of Jesus and His love.

2 I love to tell the story:
For those who know it best
Seem hungering and thirsting
To hear it, like the rest.
And when, in scenes of glory,
I sing the new, new song,
'Twill be the old, old story
That I have loved so long.

73.

1 Shall we gather at the river
Where bright angel feet have trod:
With its crystal tide forever
Flowing by the throne of God?

CHO.—Yes, we'll gather at the river,
The beautiful, the beautiful river—
Gather with the saints at the river
That flows by the throne of God.

2 On the margin of the river,
Washing up its silver spray,
We will walk and worship ever,
All the happy, golden day.

3 Ere we reach the shining river,
Lay we every burden down;
Grace our spirits will deliver,
And provide a robe and crown.

4 Soon we'll reach the shining river,
Soon our pilgrimage will cease;
Soon our happy hearts will quiver
With the melody of peace.

74.

1 Nearer, my God, to Thee,
Nearer to Thee!
E'en though it be a cross
That raiseth me;
Still all my song shall be,
Nearer, my God, to Thee,
Nearer to Thee!

2 Though, like the wanderer,
The sun gone down,
Darkness be over me,
My rest a stone,
Yet in my dreams I'd be
Nearer, my God, to Thee,
Nearer to Thee!

75.

1 Lord, I care not for riches,
Neither silver nor gold;
I would make sure of heaven,
I would enter the fold.
In the book of Thy kingdom,
With its pages so fair,
Tell me, Jesus, my Saviour,
Is my name written there?

CHO.—Is my name written there,
On the page white and fair?
In the book of Thy kingdom,
Is my name written there?

2 Lord, my sins they are many,
Like the sands of the sea,
But Thy blood, oh, my Saviour!
Is sufficient for me;
For Thy promise is written,
In bright letters that glow,
"Tho' your sins be as scarlet,
I will make them like snow."

3 Oh! that beautiful city,
With its mansions of light,
With its glorified beings,
In pure garments of white;
Where no evil thing cometh,
To despoil what is fair;
Where the angels are watching,
Yes, my name's written there.

76.

I was once far away from my Saviour,
And as vile as a sinner could be,
I wondered if Christ, my Redeemer,
Could save a poor sinner like me.

2 I wandered on in the darkness,
Not a ray of light could I see,
And the thought filled my heart with sadness,
There's no hope for a sinner like me.

3 I then fully trusted in Jesus,
And oh, what a joy came to me;
My heart was filled with His praises,
For saving a sinner like me.

4 No longer in darkness I'm walking,
For the light is now shining on me,
And now unto others I'm telling,
How He saved a poor sinner like me.

5 And when life's journey is over,
And I the dear Saviour shall see,
I'll praise Him forever and ever,
For saving a sinner like me.

77. DOXOLOGY. L. M.

Praise God, from whom all blessings flow,
Praise Him all creatures here below;
Praise Him above, ye heavenly host;
Praise Father, Son, and Holy Ghost.

78.

1 Lord Jesus, I long to be perfectly whole.
I want Thee forever to live in my soul;
Break down every idol, cast out every foe;
Now wash me, and I shall be whiter than snow.

Cho.—Whiter than snow, yes, whiter than snow; snow.
Now wash me, and I shall be whiter than

2 Lord Jesus, look down from Thy throne in the skies,
And help me to make a complete sacrifice,
I give up myself and whatever I know—
Now wash me, and I shall be whiter than snow.

3 Lord Jesus, for this I most humbly entreat;
I wait, blessed Lord, at Thy crucified feet.
By faith, for my cleansing; I see Thy blood flow— snow.
Now wash me, and I shall be whiter than

4 Lord Jesus, Thou seest I patiently wait:
Come now, and within me a new heart create;
To those who have sought Thee, Thou never said'st no— snow.
Now wash me, and I shall be whiter than

5 The blessing by faith, I receive from above;
O glory! my soul is made perfect in love;
My prayer has prevailed, and this moment I know snow.
The blood is applied, I am whiter than

79.

1 Down at the cross where the Saviour died,
Down where for cleansing from sin I cried.
There to my heart was the blood applied;
Glory to His name.

Cho.—Glory to His name,
Glory to His name;
There to my heart was the blood applied,
Glory to His name.

2 I am so wonderously saved from sin,
Jesus so sweetly abides within,
There at the cross where He took me in,
Glory to His name.

3 Oh, precious fountain that saves from sin,
I am so glad I have entered in,
There Jesus saves me and keeps me clean,
Glory to His name.

4 Come to this fountain so rich and sweet,
Cast thy poor soul at the Saviour's feet,
Plunge in to-day and be made complete,
Glory to His name.

80.

1 The great Physician now is near,
The sympathizing Jesus;
He speaks, the drooping heart to cheer,
Oh, hear the voice of Jesus.

Cho.—Sweetest note in seraph song,
Sweetest name on mortal tongue,
Sweetest carol ever sung,
Jesus, blessed Jesus.

2 Your many sins are all forgiven,
Oh, hear the voice of Jesus;
Go on your way in peace to heaven,
And wear a crown with Jesus.

3 All glory to the dying Lamb!
I now believe in Jesus;
I love the blessed Saviour's name,
I love the name of Jesus.

4 His name dispels my guilt and fear,
No other name but Jesus;
Oh, how my soul delights to hear
The precious name of Jesus.

81.

1 He leadeth me, Oh, blessed thought,
O, words with heav'nly comfort fraught,
Whate'er I do, where'er I be,
Still 'tis God's hand that leadeth me:

Ref.—He leadeth me, He leadeth me!
By His own hand He leadeth me:
His faithful follower I would be,
For by His hand He leadeth me.

2 Sometimes 'mid scenes of deepest gloom,
Sometimes where Eden's bowers bloom,
By waters still, or troubled sea,
Still 'tis His hand that leadeth me.

3 Lord, I would clasp Thy hand in mine,
Nor ever murmur nor repine,
Content, whatever lot I see,
Since 'tis my God that leadeth me.

82.

1 My hope is built on nothing less
Than Jesus' blood and righteousness;
I dare not trust the sweetest frame,
But wholly lean on Jesus' name.

Cho.—On Christ, the solid rock, I stand,
All other ground is sinking sand,
All other ground is sinking sand.

2 When darkness veils His lovely face,
I rest on his unchanging grace;
In every high and stormy gale,
My anchor holds within the vail.

Familiar Choruses.

83. HYMN.—*Come, Thou Fount of ev'ry blessing.*

Cho.—I love Jesus, Hallelujah,
I love Jesus, yes I do,
I do love Jesus, He's my Saviour,
Jesus smiles and loves me too.

84. HYMN.—*How sweet the name of Jesus sounds.*

Cho.—The half was never told,
The half was never told,
Of grace divine, so wonderful,
The half was never told.

85. HYMN.—*And can I yet delay?*

Cho.—I am coming, Lord!
Coming now to Thee,
Wash me, cleanse me, in the blood
That flowed on Calvary.

86. HYMN.—*Alas! and did my Saviour bleed?*

Cho.—The cleansing stream, I see, I see!
I plunge, and oh, it cleanseth me!
Oh praise the Lord it cleanseth me!
It cleanseth me, yes, cleanseth me!

87. HYMN.—*Jesus, Lover of my soul.*

Cho.—I am trusting, Lord, in Thee,
Blest Lamb of Calvary;
Humbly at Thy cross I bow,
Save me, Jesus, save me now.

88. HYMN.—*Jesus, my all, to heaven is gone.*

Cho.—Happy day, happy day,
When Jesus washed my sins away;
He taught me how to watch and
pray,
And live rejoicing every day;
Happy day, happy day,
When Jesus wash'd my sins away.

89. HYMN.—*Come, Thou Fount of ev'ry blessing.*

Cho.—Glory, glory, Jesus saves me,
Glory, glory to the Lamb!
Oh! the cleansing blood has reached me,
Glory, glory to the Lamb.

90. HYMN.—*Come, we that love the Lord.*

Cho.—We're marching to Zion,
Beautiful, beautiful Zion,
We're marching upward to Zion,
The beautiful city of God.

91. HYMN.—*O, when shall I see Jesus?*

Cho.—Then palms of victory, crowns of
glory,
Palms of victory, I shall wear.

92. HYMN.—*Alas! and did my Saviour bleed?*

Cho.—At the cross, at the cross where I
first saw the light,
And the burden of my heart roll'd away:
It was there by faith I received my sight,
And now I am happy all the day.

93. HYMN.—*On Jordan's banks I stand.*

Cho.—We will rest in that fair and happy
land,
Just across on the evergreen shore;
Sing the song of Moses and the Lamb by
and by,
And dwell with Jesus evermore.

94. HYMN.—*Come, ye sinners, poor and needy.*

Cho.—Turn to the Lord and seek salvation
Sound the praise of His dear name;
Glory, honor, and salvation,
Christ, the Lord, has come to reign.

95. HYMN.—*Come, Thou Fount of ev'ry blessing.*

Cho.—Now with Jesus I am rising,
On my heart his name's engrav'd;
Now my soul he is baptizing;
Glory! glory! I am saved!

96. HYMN.—*There is a fountain filled with blood.*

Cho.—Oh, glorious fountain,
Here will I stay,
And in thee ever,
Wash my sins away.

97. HYMN.—*Come, Thou Fount of ev'ry blessing.*

Cho.—All I have I leave for Jesus,
I am counting all but dross;
I am coming to the Master,
I am clinging to the cross.
Clinging, clinging, clinging to the cross.

98. HYMN.—*A charge to keep I have.*

Cho.—I'm glad Salvation's free,
I'm glad Salvation's free;
Salvation's free for you and me,
I'm glad Salvation's free.

99. HYMN.—*Alas! and did my Saviour bleed?*

Cho.—He loves me, He loves me,
He loves me, this I know;
He shed His blood on Calvary,
Because He loved me so.

100. HYMN.—*Jesus, my all, to heaven is gone.*

Cho.—Glory to God, I'm at the fountain
drinking.
Glory to God, my soul is satisfied.

INDEX.

SCRIPTURE PASSAGES

FOR USE IN

EVANGELISTIC SERVICES, THE HOME, ETC.

USE THEM FREELY.

FOR THE UNCONVERTED.

1. Are you willing to be a Christian?
   Rev. 3 : 20; Jer. 29 : 13; 1 Jno. 1 : 9; Jno. 12 : 32; Isa. 45 : 22; Jno. 3 : 14-18.

2. Are you neglecting, halting, or resisting?
   Heb. 2 : 1-3; Heb. 3 : 7-11; 1 Kings 18 : 31; Prov. 29 : 1; 2 Cor. 6 : 2.

3. Are you ashamed to confess Christ?
   Matt. 10 : 32, 33; Luke 9 : 26; Ps. 25 : 24; Rom, 1 : 16; Rom. 10 : 8-11.

4. Are you trusting in your morality, or church membership?
   Jer. 17 : 9, 10; Rom. 3 : 20-23; Jno. 16 : 8, 9; Jno. 5 : 10-13.

5. Do you say : "I'm too great a sinner?"
   Isa. 1 : 18; Isa. 43 : 25; Isa. 55 : 6, 7; 1 Tim. 1 : 15; Heb. 7 : 23; Rev. 22 : 17.

6. Are you afraid you will not find?
   Jer. 29 : 13; Matt. 7 : 7, 8; Matt. 11 : 28, 29; Isa. 45 : 19, 22; Jno. 7 : 17.

7. Do not fear you'll fall away?—Can't God keep you?
   1 Cor. 10 : 13; 2 Cor. 12 : 9; Rom. 8 : 35-39; Rom. 14 : 4 : 1 Peter 1 : 5; 2 Tim. 1 : 12; Jude 24 : 25.

8. Have you harsh views of God?
   Jno. 3 : 16; Matt. 7 : 9-11; 1 Jno. 3 : 16; Jno. 4 · 7-10, 16, 19; Rom. 5 : 6-8.

   Do not discriminate between Jesus and God the Father.
   Jno. 14 : 8, 9; 1 Tim. 3 : 16; 2 Cor. 5 : 18-21; Ps. 9 : 10.

9. Are you a scorner, or an honest doubter?
   Jno. 7 : 17; Jno. 3 : 19, 21; Jno. 19 : 15, 18, 30; Acts 17 : 11, 12; Prov. 1 : 20-23.

10. Do inconsistencies of others hinder you?
    Josh. 24 : 15; Phil. 4 : 8; Jno. 6 : 66-69; Rom. 14 : 12; Jno. 21 : 21, 22.

11. Does worldly pleasure, honor, or business prevent you?
    Matt. 6 : 33; Matt. 19 : 29, 30; Mark 8 : 36, 37; 2 Cor. 8 : 9; 1 Tim. 4 : 8.

12. Do you say : "I don't feel enough?"
    Ps. 32 : 9; Matt. 12 : 19-21; Eph. 5 : 14; Jno. 12 : 3 2; Isa. 1 : 3; Ps. 95 : 6-11.

13. Do you think it hard to live a Christian?
    Micah 6 : 8; 1 Jno. 5 : 3-5; Jno. 15 : 15; 2 Cor. 9 : 8.

14. Are you a backslider? Return now.
    Rev. 2 : 5; Hos. 14 : 4; Jer. 2 : 19; Jer. 3 : 11-14, 22; Luke 15 : 18-24.

15. Are you living in open or secret sin?
    Eccl. 8 : 11; Eccl. 9 : 18; Eccl. 11 : 9; Gal. 6 : 7, 8; Prov. 11 : 19; Prov. 28 : 13; Isa. 55 : 6, 7.

FOR CHRISTIANS.

1. Is your heart filled with love?
   1 Jno. 4 : 16-19; Mark 12 : 29-31; Eph. 3 : 17-21; Jno. 14 : 23; Rev. 3 : 20.

2. Are you doing your duty to the poor?
   Ps. 41 : 1-3; Prov. 19 : 17; 1 Tim. 6 : 17-19; Matt. 25 : 31-46.

3. Do not expect similar manifestations and details in all conversions and Christian experiences. The yielding trust and peace are the essentials.
   Acts 8 : 26-39; Acts 9 : 1-22; Acts 10 : 42-48; Acts 16 : 14, 15; Acts 25 : 34; Heb. 10 : 23; Heb. 12 : 12; Rom. 5 : 1; Isa. 26 : 3, 4.

4. Can we be certain we are saved?
   Matt. 24 : 44; 1 Cor. 2 : 12; Heb. 6 : 16-20; 1 Jno. 3 : 1, 2; Jno. 10 : 2-5, 14.

5. How may we know we are Christians?
   Rom. 5 : 1; Rom. 8 : 14-17; 1 Jno. 2 : 3; 1 Jno. 3 : 14, 24; 1 Jno. 5 : 9-12; Jno. 3 : 33.

6. Have you fears of death? Read :
   Ps. 23 : 4; Josh. 3 : 14-17; Josh. 4 : 1-18; Heb. 2 : 14, 15; 1 Cor. 15 : 55-58.

7. Have you doubts about reaching heaven?
   Luke 12 : 32; Heb. 6 : 16-20; 2 Tim. 1 : 12; Jude 24, 25.

FOR CHRISTIAN WORKERS.

1. There is a power that qualifies and disposes for work. Have you received this power?
   Acts 1 : 8; Isa. 6 : 5-8; Ps. 51 : 9-13; Luke 24 : 48, 49.

2. Have faith in God to direct and use you, though weak.
   1 Cor. 1 : 27-31; 1 Cor. 3 : 6-9; Acts 8 : 29; Dan. 12 : 3; Ps. 126 : 6; Jas. 5 : 19, 20.

3. Have unbounded faith that children and youth can be Christians.
   Prov. 22 : 6; Matt. 18 : 1-6; Mark 10 : 13-16; Eccl. 12 : 1; Jno. 21 : 15.

4. Do not argue, but invite to prove.
   Jno. 1 : 45, 46; Isa. 1 · 18; Isa. 55 : 6, 7; 1 Thess. 5 : 21; 1 Tim. 1 : 15.

5. Use God's Word and Christian experience.
   Jer. 20 : 9; Jno. 1 : 41, 45; Acts 8 : 35; Acts 26 : 9-27; 2 Tim. 3 : 15.

6. Do not tell a person he is saved. That is the Holy Spirit's work. Show how to be saved.
   1 Jno. 5 : 10; Jer. 6 : 14; 1 Cor. 2 : 10-13; Rom. 8 : 16.

7. Feel the necessity, and prove the power of prayer.
   Jer. 33 : 3; Rom. 8 : 26, 27; Jas. 5 : 16; Heb. 11 : 6.

www.ingramcontent.com/pod-product-compliance
Lightning Source LLC
Chambersburg PA
CBHW021629270326
41931CB00008B/933